SELF-ESTEEM POETRY

Inspiring Poems to Celebrate and Strengthen Womanhood

Elara F. Archer

Index

Dear Wonderful Woman,

I hope this letter finds you thriving and celebrating the essence of who you are. You are receiving this message because you, like every woman, deserve to be uplifted, acknowledged, and reminded of your inherent worth and beauty.

In a world that often tries to dictate who you should be, it's easy to forget the power of your own voice and the unique story you carry. This is an invitation to pause, breathe, and reconnect with yourself—to embrace the myriad of qualities that make you distinct and extraordinary.

Remember, your journey is yours alone, filled with strengths and triumphs that are uniquely yours. You possess a resilience that has carried you through challenges and a softness that enriches your human connections. Your life is a canvas, awaiting your vibrant colors and bold strokes.

This collection of poems, thoughts, and affirmations is crafted with you in mind, aiming to serve as gentle reminders of your capacity for love, growth, and resilience. Allow them to speak to you, comfort you, and inspire you as you navigate the beautiful complexity of life.

May you always find strength in your softness, courage in your vulnerability, and immense joy in the simple act of loving who you are. Here's to celebrating every piece of your being—may you always know how truly magnificent you are.

With all my admiration and respect,

Elara

Embrace Your Journey

Your Own Path

In the garden of life, every flower blooms at its own
    pace,
Sunlight kisses different petals, regardless of the race.
Stand tall in your beauty, unique in your frame,
For the world would be dull if every flower looked the
    same.

Reflections of Worth

Mirror on the wall, oh how you show,
Faces that change, and feelings that grow.
Yet, let me tell you what's truly divine,
It's the soul beneath that forever will shine.

Steps to Myself

With each step forward, and sometimes two back,
I learn a bit more on this unwinding track.
For every stumble and every rise,
Marks a new chapter where my strength lies.

Inner Strength

Quiet Power

Silent rivers run deep, they say,
Underneath calm, currents play.
Strength isn't loud, it need not roar,
Within your quiet, you hold the core.

Rise Again

The mighty oak feels the storm's wrath,
Yet, roots run deep in its earthen path.
Bend, it may, but never will break,
So stand strong, dear heart, with every quake.

Armor of Self

Wear your confidence as armor, bold and true,
Forge it in the fires of trials you've been through.
No foe too great, no night too dark,
Clothed in self-worth, you'll always make your mark.

Beauty Redefined

Beyond the Surface

Look beyond the surface, where true beauty lies,
Not in the mirror, but in your spirit's size.
Braver, stronger, wiser than yesterday,
Your beauty shines in your own unique way.

Infinite Variations

Not in molds, but in moments, beauty is found,
In laughter, in tears, in the silence of sounds.
You are a masterpiece designed by time,
Flawless in essence, naturally sublime.

The Art of Imperfection

Imperfect strokes create the perfect art,
Each flaw you own is a beauty part.
Celebrate each scar, each line, each spot,
For in this realness, true beauty is caught.

Self-Discovery

Map of the Soul

Explore the continents of your soul, wide and vast,
Each emotion, a river; every thought, a blast.
Discover lands within you never trod before,
In self-discovery, find oceans to adore.

Unveiling

Peel back the layers of who you think you should be,
Reveal the gem that's been there, pure and free.
In each unveiling, let the truth resonate,
That being yourself is what makes you great.

Journey Within

The longest journey you'll take is from head to heart,
From the mind's chaos to the soul's art.
Along this path, find your true essence,
In knowing yourself lies your quintessence.

Self-Love Symphony

Melody of Me

Compose the melody that sings 'I am enough,'
Play it loud when times get tough.
Your rhythm unique, your harmony light,
Dance to the beat of your heart, bright.

Echoes of Self-Love

Let the echoes of self-love fill your mind,
Gentle whispers of 'I am one of a kind.'
With each echo, let your spirits lift,
In loving yourself, you embrace life's gift.

Chorus of Care

Join the chorus that sings of self-care,
Nurturing yourself with a love so rare.
In rest and treat, in pause and play,
Find love for yourself in every day.

Claim Your Space

Stand Your Sacred Ground

Stand firm on the ground that is your own,
Claim your space, let your light be shown.
For only you can occupy your spot,
Filled with dreams that you have got.

Boundaries Bold

Set your boundaries with lines so bold,
A sacred pact with yourself uphold.
Not out of spite, nor fear, nor rage,
But from the love that comes with sage.

My Territory

This body, this mind, this soul is mine,
A universe vast, a divine design.
Respect it, cherish it, hold it dear,
For in this space, no doubt, no fear.

Empowerment Echoes

Echoes of the Mighty

Echoes of the mighty, whispers of the strong,
In your heart's chamber, they forever belong.
Summon their power, when you feel small,
You have within you, the might to stand tall.

Fires of Freedom

Ignite the fires within, let them burn bright,
A beacon of freedom, in the darkest night.
Claim your power, let no one douse,
The flames of your spirit, in your life's house.

Warrior's Call

Hear the warrior's call deep in your veins,
A song of victory, breaking all chains.
Armed with courage, shielded with grace,
March forward, in life's relentless race.

Loving Reflections

Mirror of the Mind

In the mirror of the mind, what do you see?
A reflection of what is or what could be?
Gaze deeper, past the surface, to the soul's glow,
Where love resides, let it overflow.

Self-Speak

Speak to yourself as you would to a dear friend,
With kindness and love, without pretend.
Nourish your spirit with words so sweet,
In this self-talk, let your heart beat.

Reflections Reimagined

Turn the mirror around, see yourself anew,
Reimagine a reflection that's true to you.
Not just the form, but the light within,
Reflecting love, where once was dim.

Heart's Harvest

Harvest of Happiness

Plant seeds of joy, water them with love,
In the soil of your soul, under skies above.
Harvest happiness, as it grows wild and free,
In this garden of self, let joy be the key.

Blossoms of Belief

In the heart's garden, belief blossoms bright,
Blooming in colors of immense delight.
Tend to these flowers, keep them near,
For belief in oneself clears all fear.

Fruits of Forgiveness

Forgive yourself for the paths not taken,
For dreams deferred and awakenings shaken.
Harvest the fruits of forgiveness, sweet,
A bounty of peace, no feat can beat.

Triumph of Transformation

Wings of Change

With wings of change, take flight above,
Soar through skies, pushed by self-love.
From cocoon to butterfly, embrace the shift,
In transformation, find the ultimate gift.

Metamorphosis

Each day a chance to start anew,
A metamorphosis for me and you.
Shed old skins, emerge refreshed,
In this renewal, our lives are meshed.

Triumph's Tune

Sing the tune of triumph, loud and clear,
A melody of victory, for all to hear.
Dance to the rhythm of your new-found grace,
In this transformation, find your rightful place.